Gerbils

Laura Howell

Designed by Kate Rimmer
and Adam Constantine

Illustrated by Christyan Fox
Photographs by Jane Burton
Consultant: Jackie Roswell

CONTENTS

What is a gerbil?

Gerbils are small, mouse-like animals with hairy tails and strong back legs. They are clean, fun-loving and make excellent pets. This book will tell you what you need to know about buying and taking care of your first gerbil.

Appearance

Gerbils are about 10cm (4in) tall – larger than a mouse, but smaller than a rat.

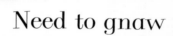

Long, sensitive whiskers

Sharp claws for digging

Powerful back legs for jumping

Although it's hard to tell here, a gerbil's tail is as long as its body. It helps the gerbil to balance.

Desert diggers

Wild gerbils and their relatives come from desert regions. They live in groups called colonies, inside huge networks of tunnels that they dig in the sand.

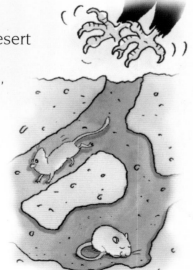

The entrance to a gerbil's tunnel is only big enough to let a gerbil through. Most enemies are too big to fit.

Need to gnaw

Like rats and hamsters, gerbils are rodents. These are animals with two pairs of strong front teeth for gnawing. The name "gerbil" comes from the Arabic word "jarbu", meaning "rodent".

Gerbils and other rodents gnaw things to keep their teeth from growing too long.

Seeing

Gerbils can see better than people in dim light, but they have trouble seeing things close up, or in great detail.

A gerbil's eyes are designed to work best in weak morning and evening light.

Smelling

Gerbils use their keen sense of smell to find food and identify friends and enemies.

Two gerbils meeting for the first time will sniff each other, to see if they are friendly.

Hearing

Gerbils have excellent hearing. When they stand up on their back legs and hold their heads high in the air, they are listening to what's going on around them.

Loud noises frighten gerbils, so keep your pet's cage in a quiet spot.

Whiskers

A gerbil uses its whiskers to detect obstacles around it, or to judge if a space is wide enough to get through. The whiskers are the same width as the body, so if they fit through a gap, the rest of the gerbil will too.

This gerbil used its whiskers to measure the width of the tunnel before crawling inside.

What will I need?

It's a good idea to have your gerbils' cage set up with everything they need before you bring your new pets home. You can buy all the items on these pages from a good pet store.

Bedding

Gerbils are natural burrowers, so they need lots of material to dig around in. Wood shavings, corn cob and straw are all suitable. You can also use sand, but it's more difficult to clean out, and must be kept damp. Don't use sawdust or cedar shavings, as they can cause infections and breathing problems.

An earthenware plant pot like this, with a little shredded paper towel inside, makes a snug gerbil hideaway.

A hideaway

Gerbils like to have a private place to go when they don't want to be disturbed. Sometimes they will just hide in their nest, but it's better for them to have a nesting box. This should be made of earthenware or wood, as plastic will be chewed up.

Nesting material

Your gerbils will want to make a nest for sleeping. Before you buy any nesting material from a pet store, check the label to make sure it is safe for gerbils. Avoid fluffy materials, such as cotton balls, as they could make your gerbil choke.

If you put a handful of toilet tissue in your gerbils' cage, they will soon shred it into a comfortable nest.

For a link to a website where you can find out whether gerbils are the right pet for you, go to **www.usborne-quicklinks.com**

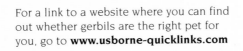

This water bottle is positioned at a comfortable height for the gerbil to drink.

Food bowls

You'll need a large, ceramic bowl for fresh and dried food. Plastic bowls are likely to get tipped over, and can be dangerous for your gerbils if they chew them.

A heavy ceramic dish is harder to tip over than a plastic one.

Water bottle

Use a drip-feed bottle for your gerbils' water, and attach it to the side of the cage or tank. Don't use a bowl, as your pets will quickly make it dirty with bedding and droppings.

Toys

Gerbils love to try out new toys. You can buy a range of gerbil toys from pet stores (see pages 24–25), but even the cardboard tube from a toilet tissue roll will provide lots of fun.

Don't clutter your gerbils' home with lots of toys. Two or three at once is enough.

A gnawing block

A gerbil needs something hard to gnaw, or its teeth will grow too long. Blocks of hard wood sold in pet stores are safest for this. Any block of clean, hard wood is suitable, though, as long as it has a smooth surface and isn't painted.

Gerbil homes

Gerbils are very active and like to dig, so they need lots of space and suitable materials to make tunnels. They can be kept in a cage, but a large glass tank will give them more freedom.

Cages

A pair of gerbils needs a cage at least 60cm (24in) long and 25cm (10in) wide. The more gerbils you have, the more room they will need. Make sure the cage has closely spaced bars that are unpainted.
Keep it where other pets, such as cats, can't reach it.

A multi-level cage has more space for playing and climbing than an ordinary one. The one shown here is large enough for toys, an exercise wheel and a hideaway.

Plastic cages

Gerbils can live in a plastic cage designed for hamsters, as long as it's big and sturdy enough. Your gerbils will enjoy running through the tunnels and connecting rooms, but you must be sure that they don't chew through the plastic.

This picture shows a multi-part plastic cage. These can be taken apart and rebuilt in different ways.

A gerbilarium

The best home for your gerbils is a large fish tank. You can fill it with enough bedding for your pets to build tunnels, and they won't be able to chew it like a plastic cage. A glass tank used to house gerbils in this way is usually called a gerbilarium.

The tank should be at least one-third full of bedding material.

This gerbilarium has been adapted to have many levels. You don't need one like this, though — a plain fish tank is fine.

Keeping covered

It's important to make sure you keep a lid on the top of the gerbilarium, or your gerbils will be able to jump out. A solid cover won't let in enough air, so use wire mesh attached to a frame made of wood or metal.

Staple chicken wire to a wooden frame to make a cover for your gerbilarium.

Staying cool

Keep the gerbilarium out of direct sunlight and away from radiators. The glass will trap heat and quickly make conditions too hot for your pets.

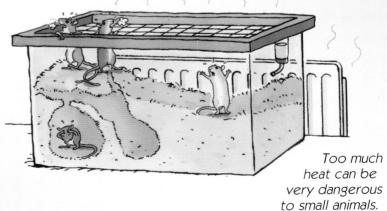

Too much heat can be very dangerous to small animals.

Choosing gerbils

It's best to buy your gerbils from a recommended pet store or breeder, who can tell you their exact age and also make sure whether they are male or female.

How many?

Gerbils don't like to live alone, so it's better to buy more than one. A pair, or a small group from the same family, will live together happily. Make sure they are all male or all female, or they will have lots of babies.

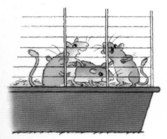

Males live happily
in groups.

Females prefer
to be in pairs.

How old?

Your gerbils should be six to eight weeks old when you buy them. They are easier to tame at this age. Before six weeks, they are too young to leave their mother.

*A breeder will not separate
baby gerbils from their
mother until they are ready.*

What to look for

*The gerbil's body should
be lean, but not bony.*

*Check that the tail is long and
straight, with no breaks or kinks.*

*The eyes should
be bright and
shiny, not dull
or sticky.*

*Make sure the nose and mouth
are dry, with no sore spots.*

*It should be clean
underneath its tail.*

*A healthy gerbil will
be active and curious.*

Mongolian gerbils

There are around 90 types of gerbils, but only a few are kept as pets. Mongolian gerbils are the easiest to take care of. They were originally bred in laboratories, but because they were so friendly and easy to take care of, they soon became popular as pets.

Jumbo jirds

Recently, people have also started keeping jirds as pets. Jirds are larger relatives of gerbils – they are about the size of a rat or small squirrel. Male jirds can be kept in pairs, but female jirds must live alone.

These are jirds. They have chubbier bodies and longer ears than Mongolian gerbils.

Buying a gerbil

1. When you go to the pet store, spend a little while just watching the gerbils in their home.

2. Decide which ones seem the most friendly and energetic. Ask if you can see them being handled.

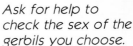

Ask for help to check the sex of the gerbils you choose.

3. Don't buy female gerbils that have been living in a cage with males. They might have babies.

9

Settling in

After you have bought your gerbils, they will need a little time to get used to their new home, and to you. On this page, you can find out how to make the move as easy as possible.

Setting up

Have a full water bottle and one day's worth of food ready in your gerbils' cage when they arrive. Ask the breeder or pet store what food they are used to eating, and buy the same kind.

A toy, like this wooden castle, will make your gerbils' home more interesting.

Coming home

Your gerbils will be put in a box when you buy them. Ask to take a little of their bedding for the new cage, so they feel more at home. Go straight home, so your gerbils won't get stressed.

A handful of bedding with a familiar scent is comforting for a gerbil.

If you have a tank, place the box inside and let the gerbils run out. Remove the box, and put the top of the tank back on. For a cage, hold the box over the open door, so the gerbils can jump inside. Close the cage door quickly.

Early days

Once you have put your gerbils in their cage, leave them alone for a day or two. They need this quiet time to get used to the sights and sounds of their new surroundings.

For a link to a website where you can find
a collection of gerbil clip-art, go to
www.usborne-quicklinks.com

Making friends

At first, your gerbils will be cautious. Talk to them often and give them small pieces of food, so they know that you're their friend.

After a few days, offer food in the palm of your hand. By now, your gerbils should be relaxed enough to step onto your hand to eat. This helps them to get used to your touch.

This gerbil is being offered a juicy raisin by its new owner.

Keep your hand still while your gerbil takes food from it.

Avoiding bites

Gerbils don't like to be grabbed roughly.

Gerbils only bite when they are very nervous or annoyed. Don't tease your gerbils by poking your fingers through the cage bars.

Try not to make quick, jerky movements or loud noises when you are near your gerbils. Never try to grab a gerbil suddenly.

Don't shout at your gerbil or punish it, even if it does bite. This will scare it, and might make it more likely to bite you again.

11

Feeding

To stay healthy, gerbils need a mixture of dried gerbil food, water, fresh vegetables and protein. (Information about fresh food is over the page.)

Pumpkin seeds

Corn

Sunflower seeds

Peanuts

Crushed dried peas

This gerbil is enjoying some sunflower seeds. You can give them as an occasional treat.

Dried food

Dried gerbil food contains a mix of things that are good for gerbils, such as dried peas, nuts and seeds. Food pellets contain the same sorts of ingredients ground up and pressed into chunks.

Gerbil food pellets come in different shapes and shades, but they are all made of the same things.

Storage

To keep your gerbil food fresh, store it in a container with a lid, in a cool, dry place. Throw food away after three months, or it will no longer be safe for your pets to eat.

Unsafe snacks

Never give a gerbil sugary foods, such as chocolate, or anything spicy or salted. All these things are bad for your pet.

Rich foods can make a gerbil fat, or sick.

Changing diet

If you find a type of food that your gerbils really like, there's no need to change it for another.

For variety, you could try giving your gerbils a new kind of food mix. You must introduce it to them gradually, or your pets might get an upset stomach.

On the first day, start by mixing about one quarter of the new food with three quarters of the old food.

Gradually add more new food and less old food over a 10-day period, until your gerbils are eating only the new food.

How much?

A full tablespoon of food, given at the same time each day, is the right amount for one gerbil. If your pets keep leaving lots of uneaten food, try giving them less. Throw the leftovers away at the end of the day.

Foraging

When you give your gerbils their food, you might see them scatter it about and pick out the pieces they like best. This is called foraging. In the wild, animals forage to find things that are safe for them to eat.

Watch your gerbil picking through its food and see if you can spot which types it likes best.

Fresh food

A small amount of fresh food is good for gerbils. Give your pets fruits or vegetables at the same time as you give them dried food.

Forbidden fruits

You should only feed your gerbils fruit once or twice a week, or they might get sick. Never give onions, lemons or oranges, or watery fruits such as melon and cucumber.

Preparing the food

Wash fruits and vegetables thoroughly in cold water before you give them to your gerbils. Dry them off, then remove the peel and seeds.

Gerbils usually like these foods.

Apple

Parsley

Radish

Broccoli

Carrot

Raisins

How much?

Give your gerbils no more than two pieces of fresh food per meal, in small chunks. Throw away any that haven't been eaten at the end of the day.

You can put fresh food in the same bowl as dried food, as shown here.

Water

Although gerbils don't drink much, they still need a regular supply of water. Fill your gerbils' water bottle with fresh water every day.

Hang the water bottle so it doesn't touch the bedding, but not too high, or your gerbils won't be able to reach the spout.

Vitamins and minerals

If a gerbil looks well and has a varied diet, it probably doesn't need extra vitamins.

Pet stores sell vitamin and mineral powders for gerbils that can be added to their food. Check the label to see if your gerbils' food contains them already.

Treats

If you'd like to give your gerbils a treat, buy one that's specially designed for rodents. Many of these treats are made with rich ingredients, so only give them to your pets occasionally.

Treat sticks contain things like raisins, popcorn and apple. They hang from the cage bars.

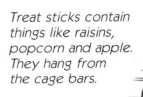

Protein

To stay healthy, gerbils need to eat food containing protein. The easiest way to add protein to your pets' diet is to give them a little cooked egg or chicken, but not too often – once every two weeks is enough.

This gerbil is about to enjoy a small piece of boiled egg.

Keeping clean

Gerbils are naturally clean animals. Because they drink so little, they don't pee much, and their droppings are very dry. This keeps their bedding from smelling bad. You still need to change it regularly, though, or it will become stale and might make your gerbils unwell.

This gerbil has been shredding its new nesting material.

Every day

Remove all uneaten food from your gerbils' food bowl, and rinse it out before putting more in. Empty and refill the water bottle.

Every week

Replace the nesting material from your gerbils' cage. You only need to change the bedding once a month.

Every two months

Make sure the top of the bucket is covered, or your gerbils will jump out.

1. Keep your gerbils in a carrying box or bucket when you clean. Put the metal part of the cage over the top.

2. Use hot water and mild dishwashing liquid to clean the water bottle, food bowl, toys and cage bottom.

3. Rinse everything off with clean water and dry it thoroughly with an old towel.

For a link to a website where you can find
more tips on how to clean out a gerbil tank,
go to **www.usborne-quicklinks.com**

Tank cleaning

Ask someone to help you take the tank outside for cleaning.

Press the bedding down firmly, so your gerbils can make sturdy tunnels.

Change dirty bedding in a tank every three months. Tank cleaning can be messy, so take it outside. Wash, rinse and dry it thoroughly.

Return the tank to its normal spot, then put in fresh bedding. Clean the food bowl and water bottle and put them back too.

Dust baths

In the desert, a wild gerbil will give itself a dust bath. It rolls around in the sand, rubbing grease off its fur. Every few weeks, give your gerbils some sand in an old dish, so they can bathe themselves.

Gerbils don't bathe in water. Instead, they bathe in rough sand, which polishes their fur.

Grooming

You don't need to wash or brush your gerbils. They clean themselves by licking their fur and running their claws and teeth through it, like a comb.

This gerbil is using its claws to groom its face and whiskers.

What does it mean?

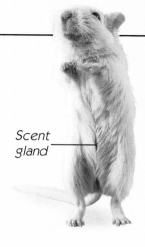

Gerbils don't make many sounds, so they use movements to let each other know how they feel. If you watch your pets carefully, you will soon learn what their body language means.

Winking

Gerbils wink when they are happy, and as a way of saying hello. If you wink at your gerbil when it's feeling friendly, it might wink back.

If your gerbil winks at you, give it a treat.

That's mine!

Gerbils have a narrow patch of bare skin called a scent gland on their tummies. This makes an oil that only gerbils can smell. They will rub the oil on anything that belongs to them.

Scent gland

Dig, dig, dig

If you see your gerbil digging furiously in the corner of its cage, don't worry. Gerbils love to dig in anything they can, so it doesn't necessarily mean your pet is trying to escape.

Gerbils can't resist the urge to dig in the corners of their home.

Face to face

When two gerbils meet, they will usually touch noses or lick each other's mouths to prove that they are friends.

These gerbils are saying hello by touching noses.

Look out!

Gerbils stamp their feet on the ground when they sense danger. This loud thumping sound warns other gerbils nearby to be on their guard. Male gerbils also thump their feet when they are excited.

An anxious gerbil makes a drumming noise with its feet.

I'm scared

Occasionally, you might hear your gerbil give out a loud, screechy squeak. Gerbils only make this noise when they are very frightened or angry. A scared gerbil will also stand perfectly still, with its front paws held up.

Frightened gerbils stand frozen on the spot, like this.

Gnawing bars

Gerbils gnaw constantly to keep their teeth worn down. If your gerbil keeps gnawing on the bars of its cage, though, it might be bored. Give it some toys to play with, and a tough wooden gnawing block.

Gerbils will gnaw anything hard. Make sure your pet has something safe to chew, or it might hurt itself by biting the cage bars.

Licking

If your gerbil is licking the sides of its tank, it may be trying to drink moisture from the glass. Check that there are no blockages in its water bottle.

Licking glass is often a gerbil's way of telling you it's thirsty.

Handling

If you want to make friends with a gerbil, you must give it lots of attention and handle it regularly. Provided you're gentle, your pets will enjoy being held in your hand.

Timing and preparation

Don't wake a sleeping gerbil up to play with it – choose a time when it's already awake, such as the early evening. Before you take your gerbil out of its cage, check that there are no cracks or holes in the walls and floorboards. Close the door, keeping all other pets out of the room.

Don't disturb your gerbils if they look sleepy.

Picking up

1. Approach your gerbil from the front, so you don't startle it. Slowly put your hand inside the cage.

2. Let the gerbil sniff your fingers. If it's happy, it will come closer, or even run onto your hand.

Hold your gerbil over a soft surface, such as a cushion, in case it jumps or falls.

3. Scoop the gerbil up using one hand on each side of its body. Gently hold it in your cupped hands.

For a link to a website with helpful hints on the right way to pick up and catch a gerbil, go to **www.usborne-quicklinks.com**

Hands off!

Most gerbils don't like having their stomachs touched. Only stroke your gerbils on their back or head.

Exploring

When your gerbil is comfortable being handled, help it get to know you better by allowing it to run up your arm and on your shoulders. Kneel down to do this, in case it jumps off.

Stroke your gerbil's back gently, as shown here, to help it feel relaxed.

Tails of woe

Gerbils have very sensitive tails, which are easily damaged. Never pick a gerbil up by its tail, especially the tip. You might pull the fur tuft off, or even snap the end.

Meeting friends

If your gerbils are completely tamed, they won't mind if other people handle them. Show your friends and family the right way to pick up and hold a gerbil before they handle them, and make sure small children don't hold them too tightly.

Help your friends when they are handling a gerbil, to make sure they do it correctly.

21

Friends and enemies

A pair or group of gerbils will be the best of friends, if they have always lived together. But if a gerbil meets a stranger, they are very likely to become enemies. An angry gerbil can give a painful bite, so if you have to handle fighting gerbils, wear thick gloves for protection.

Other pets

Although gerbils like company, don't keep them in the same cage as a hamster, mouse or other small pet. They have different habits and will probably fight.

Gerbils who are friends, like this pair, will sleep, play and eat together.

Fighting

If it's losing weight and has bite marks on its body, your gerbil might no longer be friends with its cagemate.

When gerbils fight, they rise up on their back legs and box with their front paws. Their fur bristles.

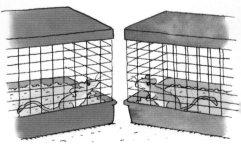

Two gerbils who have had a fight must live in separate cages afterwards, or they might hurt each other badly.

For a link to a website where you can watch
lots of video clips of gerbils, go to
www.usborne-quicklinks.com

Keep away!

Once a gerbil has decided that it owns a
particular area, it will defend it fiercely
against intruders. This area is the
gerbil's territory.

If you already have adult gerbils,
you must never try to put a new
adult in their cage. They might
accept a new young gerbil,
but it must be introduced
slowly and carefully.

*These gerbils are meeting for
the first time. They sniff to
learn each other's scents.*

Introducing a young gerbil

*Make sure the gerbils
can't wriggle under the
mesh, or through it.*

1. Thoroughly clean your
gerbil's cage and put in
fresh bedding. Place a wire
mesh panel in the middle,
dividing the cage in two.

2. Put the new gerbil on
one side of the mesh and
the older gerbil on the
other, so they can see
and smell each other.

3. Each day, switch the sides
of the mesh each gerbil is
on. After a few weeks, you
should be able to remove
the mesh completely.

Playtime

Gerbils are intelligent, energetic animals who love exploring and playing with a wide variety of toys. A bored gerbil will become grumpy and miserable, so keep your pets as busy as possible.

Wheels

If you can't let your gerbils run around outside their cage, give them an exercise wheel instead. Avoid the kind with gaps between the bars, as a gerbil's long tail can easily get damaged in them.

You can adapt a wheel with gaps to make it safe for your gerbils. Carefully wind sticky tape all around the wheel, then spread bedding on the inside, so your gerbils don't get sticky feet. Change the tape every few weeks.

A solid plastic wheel, like this one, is the safest kind for a gerbil.

Cardboard tubes

Gerbils love tunnels. Give them the cardboard middle from the inside of a roll of toilet paper or some paper towels, and they will have hours of fun running through it and chewing it to bits.

This boot-shaped toy has holes for the gerbil to poke its head through.

Playing safe

Gerbils are very inquisitive. They will investigate anything, even if it's not safe.

1. You can let your gerbil out to run around, as long as you watch it closely. Keep it away from dangers such as hot radiators, electric cables, and liquids.

2. Warn people when your gerbil is out of its cage, so it doesn't get hurt accidentally. If you have lots of gerbils, it's safer to have only one out at once.

Exercise balls

Exercise balls are useful if you don't have a room where your gerbils can safely run free.

It's easier to keep a close eye on your gerbil when it's out of its cage if you let it run around in a clear plastic exercise ball. Don't let it spend more than about 10 or 15 minutes in the ball, or it might become exhausted.

Finding lost gerbils

If a gerbil escapes and you don't know which room it's in, put four sunflower seeds on the floor of each one. Close the doors, and see which seeds get eaten.

Sunflower seeds can usually lure lost gerbils out of hiding.

Baby gerbils

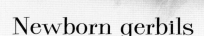

Baby gerbils are called pups. A pair of male and female gerbils will have pups if they live together. It's best you don't let this happen, because you'll need to find homes for all the pups afterwards. Just one pair of gerbils could produce over eighty pups in a year.

This is what a nest of newborn gerbils looks like.

Separated parents

In the wild, gerbil parents stay together to look after their pups. Pet gerbil parents should be kept apart before the birth, though.

If you don't separate the parents, they will keep having more pups.

The new mother

Female gerbils give birth to their pups after 24 days. A mother gerbil can have up to seven pups at once.

Newborn gerbils

Newborn gerbils are about the size of a grape. They have no hair, and they can't see or hear. For the first few weeks, the pups stay huddled in the nest with their mother. She licks them clean and feeds them milk.

A mother gerbil cares for her pups.

Tiny explorers

Although they are blind, gerbil pups like to crawl around and explore. Their mother picks them up gently in her mouth and returns them to the nest if they stray too far.

These lively pups are just over one week old.

Growing up

The pups change quickly. Within two weeks, their fur has grown, their eyes are starting to open, and they can hear and run. At this age, they love to chase and wrestle with each other.

Pups like to play-fight, but they don't hurt each other.

Becoming parents

Gerbils can have pups of their own when they are only eight weeks old. To avoid this, the brothers and sisters must be separated from each other, and from their parents, after six weeks.

This six-week-old gerbil already looks like a mini version of its mother.

Keeping healthy

Well-cared-for gerbils will rarely become sick. If you suspect something is wrong with your gerbil, you might be able to treat it at home, although some problems will need a vet.

Bald spots

Gerbils sometimes develop bald spots around their noses. This is usually caused by the gerbil rubbing its face against the cage bars. If the skin looks red and runny, though, your pet might be allergic to its bedding, so try using a different kind.

If your gerbil rubs its nose a lot, like this, it might have an allergy.

Pests

Tiny creatures called mites get in an animal's fur and make it itch. If you see something moving in your gerbil's fur, or it has sore skin, go to a pet store and buy lotion designed to kill these pests. You must also wash the cage or tank with hot, soapy water, and replace the bedding.

These mites are drawn close up, but they're too small to see in real life. Check for sore patches of skin instead.

A damaged tail

Gerbils' tails are fragile, and can be damaged easily. Picking up a gerbil by its tail might cause the skin or hairy tuft on the end to come off. Broken tails heal quickly, but they will never grow back to their full length.

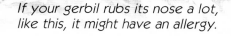

A gerbil can survive losing part of its tail, but it will find it a little harder to balance.

For a link to a website where you can find more
information about gerbil health problems,
go to **www.usborne-quicklinks.com**

Signs of sickness

*Refusing food might
mean that your
gerbil is sick.*

*A gerbil with a cold will
sneeze and have trouble
breathing.*

*Watery droppings
are usually a sign of
an upset tummy.*

A gerbil that doesn't want
to eat and has ruffled fur
might be unwell. Keep it
warm and let it rest quietly.

If your gerbil's breathing
makes a clicking sound, it
probably has a cold. Take
it to a vet right away.

Gerbil droppings should
look dry. If they become
runny, feed your gerbil only
dried food for a few days.

Weight problems

A gerbil that eats too much
and exercises too little will
get fat. But if your gerbil is
getting thinner, problems
with its teeth might be
stopping it from eating
properly. Overgrown teeth
can be clipped, and broken
teeth will grow back.

*Give an overweight
gerbil low-fat
foods, such as
dried peas.*

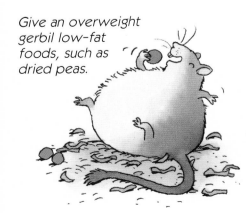

Older gerbils

As they get older,
gerbils sleep more
and become less
active. When your
gerbil reaches
three years old,
start adding a little
vitamin powder to
its food to help it
stay healthy.

*With a healthy diet
and lots of exercise,
your gerbil could
live to be five years
old, like this one.*

Going to the vet —

If your gerbil becomes sick and doesn't begin to recover by itself, it will need a trip to the vet.

This gerbil is being sprayed with an anti-flea treatment.

The vet gently holds the gerbil by the base of its tail while she sprays its body.

What will the vet do?

Depending on what's wrong with your pet, the vet might give it an injection, or some medicine. Vets can also treat gerbils that have skin problems, or pests in their fur.

On the move

Take your gerbil to the vet in a small, plastic carrying box. A cardboard box is not suitable, because your gerbil will be able to chew through it.

A little bedding or paper in the carrying box makes it more comfortable.

Teething troubles

If your gerbil's teeth have become overgrown, ask the vet to clip them. Overgrown teeth could harm your pet.

A gerbil's teeth grow too long if it doesn't have enough hard things to gnaw.

Going away

When you go away for a while, you must make sure your gerbils stay safe and well. Gerbils can be left alone for a short time, but if you're going away for more than two nights, ask a friend to look after your pets.

A short break

If you're only away for a night or two, clean the gerbils' cage or tank and replace all the bedding. Fill the water bottle, and leave enough dry food to last until you return. Don't leave fresh food, as it will spoil.

This jird is enjoying having a peanut as a treat while its owner is away.

Gerbilsitting

It's easier to ask someone you trust to visit your home, rather than trying to take a tank or large cage to them.

Leave your friend everything she will need to look after your pets. Tell her what sorts of food they can have.

Make sure your friend knows what to do if a gerbil escapes, and give her the phone number of a local vet.

Index

Cover design by Michael Hill

With thanks to Donna Bennett